Focus on the SEASONS

Focus on
WINTER

By Rosie Seaman

Fearon Teacher Aids
Simon & Schuster Supplementary Education Group

ABOUT THE AUTHOR

Rosie Seaman is an educator, author, and television producer. She has written several books for children and her work has been highlighted in a number of national magazines. As director of children's programming for WKRG-TV in Mobile, Alabama, Ms. Seaman has developed a variety of educational programs for young children.

Ms. Seaman received her certification in the Montessori method of preschool education and bases her work on the Montessori philosophy that young children learn best through techniques that encourage manipulation, experimentation, and discovery of the world around them.

Editorial Director: Virginia L. Murphy

Editors: Marilyn Trow and Sue Mogard

Copyeditor: Lisa Schwimmer

Design: Terry McGrath

Production: Rebecca Speakes

Cover Design: Lucyna Green

Cover and Inside Illustration: Marilynn Barr

ISBN 0-86653-971-9

Contents

A Note from the Author

The *Focus on the Seasons* series teaches basic skills, concepts, and subject matter to young children through active participation and discovery. Arranged in four seasonal books, the activities offer young learners the opportunity to express themselves freely throughout the school year as they contribute to their school environment.

Focus on Winter helps children discover some of the seasonal changes of winter, share information about their families, learn to help others using newly acquired skills, enjoy winter through art, and celebrate the winter holiday season.

Invite the children to help set up an area in the classroom for sharing completed projects about winter. For example, a specific wall space and table may be used to display the children's creations. Displaying children's work is important to reinforce visually the skills and concepts they learn each day.

Use this book as a way of opening many other exciting avenues for exploring winter with the children. The results will be an accumulation of endless treasures that will always be of great value to both you and your young students. Have fun together!

Rosie Seaman

Introduction

The *Focus on the Seasons* series encourages you, the teacher, to be actively involved with the children and their learning. Each seasonal book provides children with an opportunity to learn about the seasons, as well as one another, through hands-on experiences with a variety of materials.

The format of each book offers easy reference to activities that explore commonly used early-childhood units, as well as suggesting a hands-on approach for implementing the activities into existing programs. Each book presents simple directions and bold illustrations and includes a bibliography of quality children's books to enhance the seasonal themes.

The activities begin with a list of materials to gather and offer suggested discussion questions. Each activity provides a step-by-step process for involving the children and suggests other alternatives when appropriate.

A SUGGESTED APPROACH

Prior to each activity:

➤ invite the children into the activity with the discussion questions, expanding the ideas presented in the questions as the children show interest.

➤ display the suggested materials on a low table in a work area that encourages the children to work independently.

During each activity:

➤ encourage the children to express their unique ideas through the materials.

➤ become involved with the children through conversations or mutual participation in the projects.

Following each activity:

➤ place the materials in a learning center in the classroom for the children to explore during independent time.

➤ display the children's completed creations in the classroom for you and the children to enjoy.

OBSERVING THE CHANGES OF WINTER

WINTER is a season filled with many changes. Through hands-on activities, the children will discover changes in the weather, discuss popular winter activities, explore the properties of snow, and learn about other visual changes in nature.

A Winter Scene

MATERIALS

➤ black sheets of construction paper

➤ colored chalk

➤ glue

➤ salt

➤ newspapers

SHARING TOGETHER

➤ What do you like best about winter? How is winter different from fall? Can you tell me about winter weather? What do you see outside in the winter?

➤ Can you describe snow? How does snow feel? Have you ever looked closely at a snowflake? Can you describe a snowflake? What can you make out of snow?

WORKING TOGETHER

Invite the children to make a winter scene. Give each child a black sheet of construction paper and place the other materials listed on page 8 within easy reach of the children. Show the children how to squeeze an ample amount of glue on the construction paper and then use their fingers to spread the glue on the areas in their pictures where they want snow to appear. Help the children sprinkle salt over the glue, covering it fully. Wait for the glue to dry and then have the children hold their pictures over a work table covered with newspaper. Shake off any excess salt (the salt may be collected and reused). Encourage the children to use colored chalk to draw in other details for their snow pictures as well. Display the children's pictures on a "Winter Wonderland" bulletin board.

Snowball Game

MATERIALS

➤ cotton balls
➤ rulers

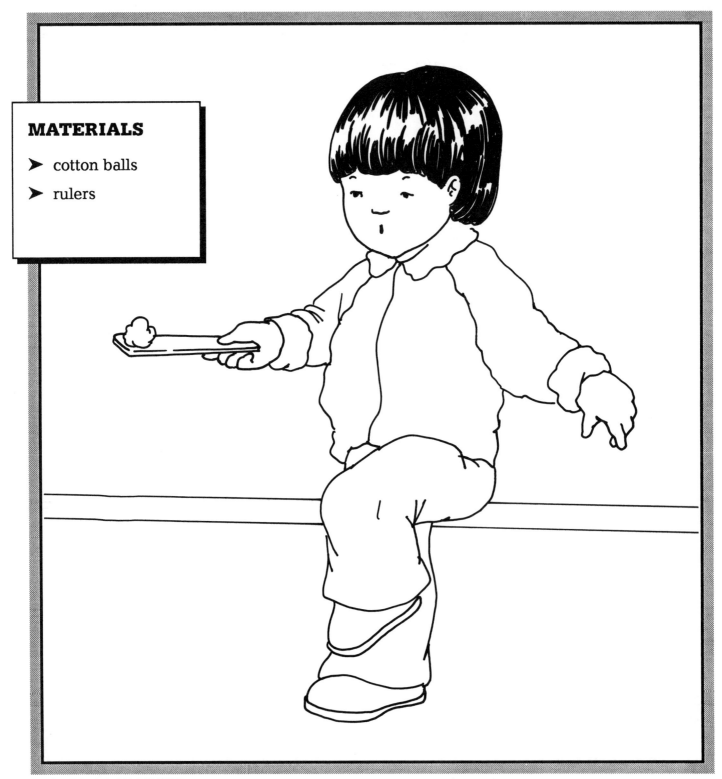

SHARING TOGETHER

➤ What is snow made of? What can you make out of snow? What games do you like to play in the snow? Have you ever made snow angels? Let's pretend to make snow angels in the snow. (If possible, take the children outside on a snowy day and make real snow angels.)

➤ Can you make a pretend snowball and balance it carefully on your hand? How about your foot? Your elbow? How about your forehead?

WORKING TOGETHER

Give each child a cotton ball and a ruler. Ask the children what they think a cotton ball looks like. Explain that the children will be playing a balancing game with several "snowballs." Invite the children to balance the cotton balls on the ends of the rulers while following the directions below. Remind the children to do their best to keep the cotton ball snowballs on their rulers as they follow the directions. Encourage the children to take turns being the leader and giving directions for the other children to follow.

Turn around in a circle.

Balance on one foot and then the other foot.

Hold the ruler and "snowball" above your head.

Exchange rulers with another child.

Walk over and touch a wall and then walk back to your place.

As an alternative to this activity, have the children play a relay game with the rulers and cotton balls. Divide the class into two teams and have the children pass the ruler and cotton ball down the line. If the children drop the cotton ball, they may pick it up and resume the game. The team that passes the cotton ball to the end of the line first wins the game.

A Snowperson

MATERIALS

➤ marshmallows (regular size and miniature)

➤ gumdrops

➤ toothpicks

➤ scissors

SHARING TOGETHER

➤ What is snow? How is snow made? Have you ever played in the snow? What did you do? Did you make a snowball? Let's pretend to make snowballs together.

➤ Do you know how to make a snowperson? How? Raise your hand if you have ever made a snowperson. Did you make eyes for your snowperson? What did you use to make the eyes? How about a nose? Mouth? What did you use to make the nose and mouth for your snowperson?

WORKING TOGETHER

Invite the children to wash their hands and a working surface thoroughly before handling any food items. Set the materials listed here within easy reach of the children. Ask the children if they know how they can make a snowperson using these materials. Show the children how they can use toothpicks to fasten the flat sides of the large marshmallows together to make the snowperson's body. Then demonstrate for the children how to make arms for the snowpeople by attaching toothpicks on the sides of the middle marshmallows. Invite the children to put miniature marshmallows on the toothpicks. Cut gumdrops into small pieces and then help the children press the sticky sides on the marshmallows to create facial features, buttons, or other details.

ALL ABOUT MY FAMILY

THE FAMILY is an integral part of a child's life. In this section, children discuss what is special about their families, as well as create art projects emphasizing the uniqueness of their family members. Be sure to remain sensitive to each child's different family situation.

Family Portrait Gallery

MATERIALS

- ➤ paper plates
- ➤ marking pens or crayons
- ➤ yarn (yellow, black, brown, red, gray)
- ➤ stapler
- ➤ glue
- ➤ scissors
- ➤ ribbon
- ➤ fabric scraps

SHARING TOGETHER

➤ How many people do you have in your family? Can you name all of the people in your family? How many girls are in your family? How many boys? How many older people are in your family?

WORKING TOGETHER

Explain to the children that they are going to make a winter portrait gallery of their families. Staple together as many paper plates in a row as there are people in each child's family. Place the other materials listed on page 14 on a work table within easy reach of the children. Make sure the children include themselves in the portraits, too. Be sensitive to each child's unique family situation. Encourage children with foster families, those living with other relatives, friends, and so on, to include any or all of these people in their galleries. Invite the children to use marking pens or crayons to draw faces on the plates to represent each member of their families. Encourage the children to glue appropriate colors of yarn on the plates for hair. Invite the children to make winter hats or scarves using fabric scraps and include them on their portraits as well. Staple loops of ribbon to the top plates for hanging in a classroom display, or the children may take their winter portraits home for their families to enjoy.

Family Placemats

MATERIALS

➤ crayons

➤ white construction paper

➤ scissors

SHARING TOGETHER

➤ What kinds of foods do you like to eat in the winter? Do you like to eat warm foods or cold foods? What foods warm you up in the winter? Do you like to eat soup? How about popsicles? Do you ever have hot drinks in the winter? How about hot cocoa?

➤ Do you sit in a special seat at mealtime? How do you help your family at mealtime? Do you help set the table? Clear the table? What other things do you do to help your family at mealtime?

WORKING TOGETHER

Invite the children to make special placemats for their families. Give each child a piece of white construction paper. Place the crayons and scissors on a work table within easy reach of the children. Ask the children to draw pictures of their families on the construction paper. Have the children write the names of the family members under each of their pictures with the help of an adult volunteer. Then show the children how to fringe the edges of their papers using a scissors. Encourage the children to enjoy using the family placemats at snacktime and sharing with others about the members of their families. Or, invite the children to take their placemats home to share with their families.

Family Poster

MATERIALS

- ➤ long sheet of white butcher paper
- ➤ old magazines
- ➤ glue
- ➤ scissors

HOORAY FOR OUR FAMILIES!

SHARING TOGETHER

➤ What does your family like to do together? Have you ever taken a family vacation or trip? Tell us about it.

➤ Why are families important? What things do you like to do with your family? What special winter activities do you like to do with your family? Have you ever gone sledding with your family? How about skating? Tell us about a special winter activity you do with your family.

WORKING TOGETHER

Before beginning this activity, print "Hooray for Our Families" in large letters across the top of a long sheet of white butcher paper. Then invite the children to make a classroom family poster. Encourage the children to cut out pictures from old magazines of families doing activities together. Show the children how to glue the pictures on a large sheet of butcher paper. Display the poster and discuss with the children the activities represented.

As an alternative activity, invite the children to make individual collages of family activities they like to do. Encourage the children to cut pictures from old magazines of family activities and glue the pictures on sheets of construction paper. The children can take their collages home to share with their families.

Winter Family Fun

MATERIALS

➤ paper plates

➤ marking pens or crayons

SHARING TOGETHER

➤ Name something that you and your family like to do on a winter day. Do you like to play in the snow together? Build a snow fort? Drink hot cocoa? If you could do anything with your family on a snowy day, what would you like to do?

WORKING TOGETHER

Invite the children to make pictures of family activities. Give each child a paper plate. Have the children draw pictures of their families having fun together on a winter day. Be sure to remain sensitive to different family situations. Suggest to the children that they decorate the edges of the plates to make frames. Encourage the children to share their family fun pictures, noting similarities and differences in family interests. Display the pictures on a bulletin board entitled "Winter Family Fun!"

BEING A HELPER

B Y WINTERTIME, children often begin to shift their focus on self to an awareness of belonging to a group. Helping others is an important way for children to feel they contribute and belong. The following activities encourage children to explore ways of helping others and learn about the many ways our hands help us every day.

Helper Poster

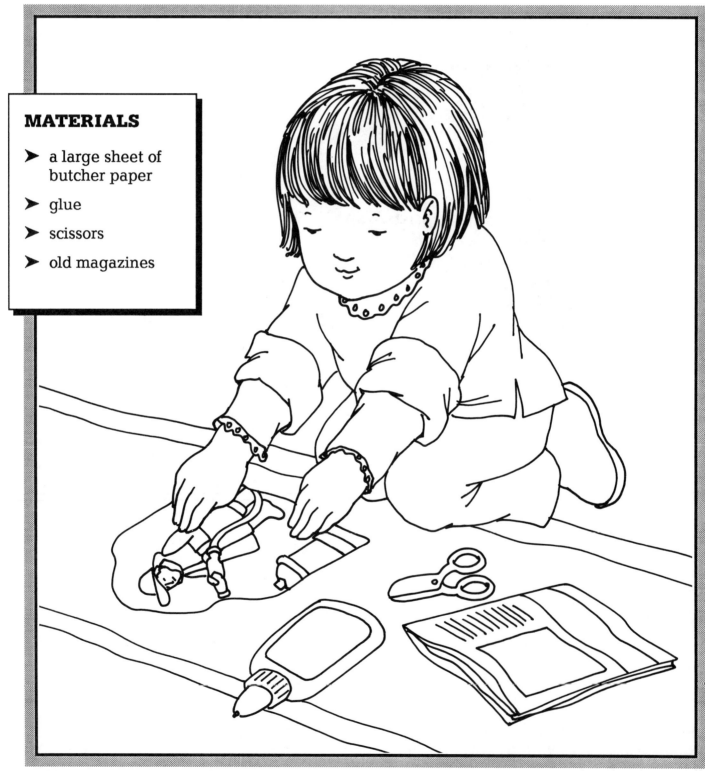

MATERIALS

➤ a large sheet of butcher paper

➤ glue

➤ scissors

➤ old magazines

SHARING TOGETHER

➤ What do you do to help at home? Raise your hand if you have ever helped shovel the walk at home. Have you ever helped a friend make a snowperson? How else have you helped someone? What are some ways you help at school? Can you name some ways other people help you? How does it make you feel to help someone?

WORKING TOGETHER

Invite the children to make a helper poster for the classroom. Encourage the children to cut out pictures from old magazines of people helping one another. Help the children glue the pictures onto a long sheet of butcher paper. Display the poster in the classroom. Discuss the many ways people help one another.

Helpful Items

MATERIALS

➤ a large box containing a variety of helpful items—bandages, broom, hammer, flowers, snow shovel, and so on

➤ crayons

➤ drawing paper

SHARING TOGETHER

➤ Do you clean your room? Do you share a room with a brother or sister? Do you help each other keep your room clean? How? What items do you use to clean your room? Do you know how to fold your clothes and put them away? Let's pretend to put away our clothes together. Have you ever helped sweep or vacuum the floor in your room? Let's pretend to sweep and vacuum together. What other chores do you help with at home? Do you pick up litter in the yard?

WORKING TOGETHER

Invite the children to take turns selecting objects from a large box labeled "Helpful Items." Then ask each child to share with the rest of the class how the items might be used to help other people. Ask the children to name some special helpful items they might use in the winter. Encourage the children to think of other helpful items that might be added to the box as well. As an addition to this activity, invite the children to draw pictures of themselves doing a helpful activity at home or at school.

Create with Your Hands

SHARING TOGETHER

➤ How many fingers do you have on one hand? Two hands? Can you name some helpful jobs you can do for others with your hands?

➤ What does the shape of your hand remind you of? Can you think of an animal that your hand looks like? How about an object? What do you think you could make using your handprint?

WORKING TOGETHER

Invite the children to make special winter pictures using their hands. Give each child a sheet of white construction paper. Ask the children to lay their hands flat on the construction paper and then use crayons to trace around their hands with the help of an adult volunteer. Then invite the children to draw details on the hand outlines to make winter pictures of animals or objects. Encourage the children to be creative. Display the hand pictures in the classroom to show the different ways hands may be used to create special drawings.

As an alternative activity, divide the class into student pairs and encourage the children to take turns helping each other trace around their hands. Another way to do a helpful job with helping hands!

Helping Hands Banner

MATERIALS

➤ construction paper in a variety of colors

➤ crayons

➤ glue

➤ long sheet of white butcher paper

➤ scissors

SHARING TOGETHER

➤ Do you help your friends? Have you ever helped a friend build a snowperson? How about a snow fort? Tell us about a time when you helped a friend. Let's all help each other make a Helping Hands Banner.

WORKING TOGETHER

Before beginning this activity, print "Helping Hands" in large letters across the top of a long sheet of white butcher paper. Then give each child a sheet of construction paper in a color of their choice. Encourage the children to use crayons to trace around their hands on the construction paper, or invite the children to help each other trace one another's hands. Help the children cut out their hand outlines and write their names on their hand shapes. Show the children how to glue their paper hands on the long sheet of butcher paper. Display the banner on a classroom wall. Help the children compare the different sizes and shapes of hands.

LEARNING NEW SKILLS

CHILDREN gain confidence in themselves as they learn new skills and apply them daily. The following activities provide opportunities for the children to expand their imaginations, develop memory recall, distinguish rhyming sounds, sort items, arrange numbers in order, compare items according to various attributes, and develop number sense.

Share a Thought

MATERIALS

➤ white drawing paper

➤ marking pens or crayons

➤ scissors

SHARING TOGETHER

➤ What do you think about on a cold winter day? Can you tell me one of your favorite thoughts? Did you know that when you think about something, no one knows what you're thinking about? Thoughts are private. People only know what you are thinking about if you tell them. Would anyone like to share a special winter thought?

WORKING TOGETHER

Give each child a sheet of drawing paper. Invite the children to draw large cloud shapes and then color pictures of their favorite thoughts inside the clouds. Encourage the children to share their drawings with the class. Help the children cut out their clouds and display their special thoughts around the classroom or on a Sharing Wall.

Design Time

MATERIALS

➤ colored paper, torn into pieces

➤ glue

➤ black construction paper

➤ crayons or marking pens

SHARING TOGETHER

➤ Close your eyes and imagine a fun place to play. What does this place in your mind look like? Can you describe it for us? What would you play at this place in your mind? Do you know what your imagination is? How is your imagination helpful to you? Your imagination helps you make up things to think about. In your imagination, you can make anything happen. Did you know that everyone has an imagination?

WORKING TOGETHER

Invite the children to use their imaginations to make a special, colorful winter design. Give each child a sheet of black construction paper. Place the other materials listed on page 32 on a work table within easy reach of the children. Suggest that the children experiment making several different designs with the colored pieces of paper. Then help the children glue their best designs on the black construction paper. Encourage the children to add to their creative winter designs with crayons or marking pens, if they wish.

Recall Game

MATERIALS

➤ buttons in a
   variety of
   different shapes,
   sizes, and colors

SHARING TOGETHER

➤ Do you wear a coat in the winter? How do you keep your coat closed when it is cold? Raise your hand if you have buttons on your coat. Can you button your coat?

➤ Show the children several buttons. Can you point to the buttons that are red? Green? Blue? Yellow? Which buttons have four holes in them? Which buttons have two? Which button is your favorite? Why?

WORKING TOGETHER

Invite the children to sit together with you in a circle on the floor to play a button game. Place five buttons in a row on the floor in the center of the circle. Touch one of the buttons. Then invite one child to touch that button again and then touch another button. Invite another child to touch these two buttons and another button of his or her choice. Continue with the activity until all of the children in the group have had a turn to touch the buttons. For a special challenge, add more buttons and go around the group more than once. Continue as long as the children show interest.

I Can Remember

MATERIALS

➤ none

SHARING TOGETHER

➤ Do you know what the word *remember* means? When you remember something, that means you think of it again. Do you remember what you had for breakfast today? What did you have? Do you remember what season comes before winter?

➤ What things do you need to remember? Do you need to remember to do certain chores around the house? Does someone in your family help you to remember things? Who?

WORKING TOGETHER

Explore questions like the following that reinforce the children's abilities to associate time, develop memory, and express themselves verbally.

"What was the first thing you did today after breakfast?"

"What are two things you did before coming to school?"

"Who brought you to school today?"

"Name two things you saw on the way to school."

"What did you enjoy most today at school?"

"What is your bedtime?"

Rhyming Word Match

MATERIALS

➤ pictures of items that have rhyming names, such as a car and a jar, a chick and a stick, and so on

➤ glue

➤ index cards

SHARING TOGETHER

➤ Do you know what the word *rhyme* means? Did you know that words that rhyme are words that sound alike? Sing "Row, Row, Row Your Boat." What words in the song sound alike?

➤ Can you name a word that rhymes with the word *car*? What winter word rhymes with the word *bow* (snow)? What winter word rhymes with the word *red* (sled)? Look around the classroom and find something that rhymes with the word *floor*. Hint: I came through the (door).

WORKING TOGETHER

Before beginning this activity, glue each rhyming picture on an index card. Then invite the children to play a rhyming word match game. Ask the children to sit together with you in a circle on the floor. Invite the children to look at each picture you show them and identify the items. Encourage the children to take turns matching the pictures with other pictures of items that have rhyming names.

Big and Little

MATERIALS

➤ pictures of a small and a large object

➤ a large box containing different items of varying sizes, such as a spool of thread, a ball, gloves, shoes, and so on

➤ 2 sheets of white poster paper

➤ glue

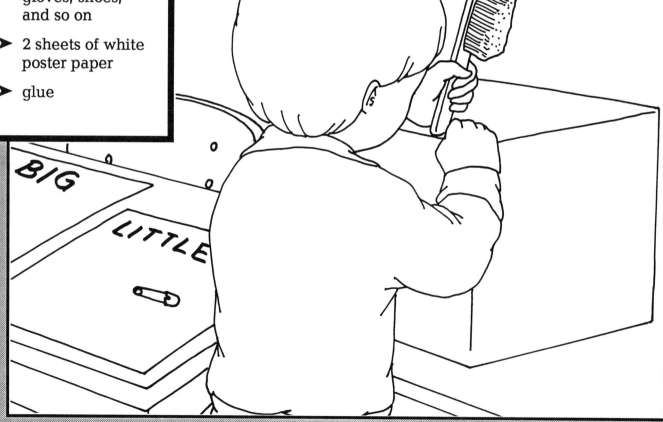

SHARING TOGETHER

➤ Can you name something that is bigger than a chair? What can you make in the snow that is big (snowperson, snow fort, snow angel)? Name something you are bigger than. Are you bigger than a table? Are you bigger than a mouse? Can you make yourself bigger? Let's try together. Stand up and stretch your arms over your heads. Now you're bigger!

➤ Can you name something that is smaller than a cup? Can you name something smaller than your hand? Look at your thumb. Look at your foot. Which is bigger? Name something small you can make out of snow (snowball). Can you make yourself smaller? Let's try it. Roll up into a ball on the floor. Make yourself as small as you can.

WORKING TOGETHER

Before beginning this activity, print "Big" in large letters across the top of one large sheet of poster paper and "Little" across the top of the other sheet. Glue a picture of a small object on the poster paper labeled "Little" and a picture of a large object on the poster paper labeled "Big." Then invite the children to play a big and little game. Encourage the children to take turns removing two items from a large box containing different items of varying sizes. Then invite each child to place the items on the appropriate posters according to size. Ask the children to contribute items from home that may be added to the box as well.

As an extension to this activity, invite the children to cut out pictures of big and little items from magazines. Then encourage the children to glue the big and little pictures on the appropriate sheets of poster paper and display the posters in the classroom. Pictures may be added throughout the unit for continued recognition of "big" and "little."

Shapes and Sizes

MATERIALS

➤ pictures of winter objects shaped like rectangles, circles, squares, and triangles, such as a sled (rectangle), snowball (circle), cap (triangle), and shovel (square)

➤ felt rectangles, squares, circles, and triangles of the same color

➤ flannelboard

SHARING TOGETHER

➤ Show the children winter items of different shapes, such as those listed on page 42. Let's look at these winter items. Can you find a winter item shaped like a (circle)? (Continue playing the game, pointing out the different shapes in winter objects.)

➤ Can you find something in this room that is shaped like a circle? Can you find something in this room that is shaped like a triangle? A square? A rectangle? How is a rectangle different from a square?

WORKING TOGETHER

Invite the children to play a sorting game. Place the felt shapes randomly on a flannelboard. Then ask the children to come up, one at a time, and sort the different felt shapes on the flannelboard according to shape and size. Make sure each child gets a chance to sort the shapes. Encourage the children to use the felt shapes to make patterns and designs on the flannelboard as well. Suggest that the children take turns making flowers, houses, faces, and so on. Store the materials in a box with a smaller flannelboard in a learning center for the children to work with during independent time.

Number and Value

SHARING TOGETHER

➤ Hold up one mitten. How many mittens am I holding? How many mittens do you think you need to wear to play outside in the wintertime? (Hold up all four mittens.) How many mittens am I holding now? How many children can go outside and play in the snow with this many mittens?

➤ Can you count from one to ten? Can you point to the plate with the number 5 written on it? Can you clap your hands three times?

WORKING TOGETHER

Before beginning this activity, print a numeral from one to ten on each of ten paper plates. Then invite the children to play a number matching game. Ask the children to help arrange the paper plates in numerical order. Count out loud with the children as they arrange the plates. Suggest that the children try arranging the paper plates in numerical order without your help as well. Then encourage the children to take turns placing an appropriate number of counters on each plate. Encourage the children to count out loud as each counter is placed.

As an alternative activity, draw dots on the plates to correspond to the numerals. The children may then place one marker on each of the dots to complete the activity. Or, invite the children to arrange the plates in order from one to ten and then choose a plate and clip on to the plate a corresponding number of clothespins.

Weigh and Compare

MATERIALS

➤ a large box containing different items of varying weights, including a feather and a brick

➤ scale

SHARING TOGETHER

➤ Here is a feather. Here is a brick. Which do you think is heavier? Which do you think is heavier—a snowball or a snowflake? Find something in the room that is light enough for you to carry. Find something that is too heavy for you to carry. Do you think you can carry an elephant? How about a kitten?

WORKING TOGETHER

Invite the children to play a comparison game. Explain to the children the meaning of the words *heavier* and *lighter*. Then ask the children to sit together with you in a circle on the floor. Encourage each child to select two items at a time from a large box containing different items of varying weights. Ask the children to compare the weights of the items. Ask each child which item they think is heavier. Then place each item on a scale to check the children's predictions.

As an alternative activity, challenge the children to predict how much each item will weigh. Children will be surprised by their guesses and the actual weights. Continue if children remain interested.

Sorting Buttons by Size

MATERIALS

➤ buttons of the same color in varying sizes

➤ 3 bowls or plastic containers

small

medium

large

SHARING TOGETHER

➤ Can you find a small button? Now try to find a large button. Can you find two buttons that are the same size? Find a small, medium-size, and large button. Can you put the buttons in order from smallest to largest? Let's try it.

➤ Can you find two items in the classroom that are the same size? What do you wear in the winter that has buttons (coat, sweater)?

WORKING TOGETHER

Gather the children together around a work table. Spread out a variety of buttons. Ask the children to examine the buttons carefully and then take turns sorting the buttons according to size. Then invite the children to sort the small, medium-size, and large buttons and place them in separate bowls or plastic containers.

As an extension of this activity, invite the children to sort buttons according to size with their eyes shut (or provide a loose-fitting blindfold) and use only their sense of touch.

Sorting Buttons by Color

MATERIALS

➤ buttons of the same size in varying colors, especially primary and secondary colors

SHARING TOGETHER

➤ Can you find something in the classroom that is the same color as this button? (Hold up a solid color button.) Do you have buttons on your winter coat or on a sweater? What color are the buttons on your coat or sweater?

➤ Can you find two buttons that are the same color? Try to find two red buttons. Now can you find two blue buttons? What is your favorite color? Can you find a button that is that color?

WORKING TOGETHER

Gather the children together around a work table. Spread a variety of colored buttons on the table. Ask the children to examine the different buttons and then sort the buttons according to color. Invite the children to continue a color pattern you start with the buttons, such as alternating red and blue buttons, and so on. Or, children may create their own color patterns.

Box-a-Button Game

MATERIALS

➤ buttons

➤ a large box

➤ white paper

➤ masking tape

➤ crayons or
marking pens

SHARING TOGETHER

➤ Count how many buttons I throw into a box (throw in
two buttons). Count with me as I throw five buttons
into a box. (Continue throwing buttons into the box
and have the children count with you each time.)

WORKING TOGETHER

Set the materials listed here, except for the buttons, on
a work table within easy reach of the children. Help the
children tape white paper to the sides of a large box.
Encourage the children to use crayons or marking pens to
draw ten winter objects on the box.

Then invite the children to play a button game. Place
the decorated box in a designated area in the classroom.
Set down a strip of masking tape a foot or so away from
the box. Ask each child, one at a time, to step up to the
tape line. Hand the child ten buttons and invite the child
to throw the buttons, one at a time, into the box. Encourage
the children to count the number of buttons they successfully
throw into the box. After each child has had a turn,
challenge the children to keep trying to get more buttons
into the box. Encourage the children to try to get all the
buttons into the box.

ENJOYING SPECIAL WINTER DAYS

CHILDREN gain information about their heritage and the heritage of others by celebrating special holidays with family and friends. During the following activities, the children explore customs associated with the winter holiday season, prepare and eat holiday foods, and make several holiday decorations.

A Holiday Bouquet

MATERIALS

➤ 4-inch paper doilies (round)

➤ pipe cleaners (cut in half)

➤ gumdrops

➤ crayons

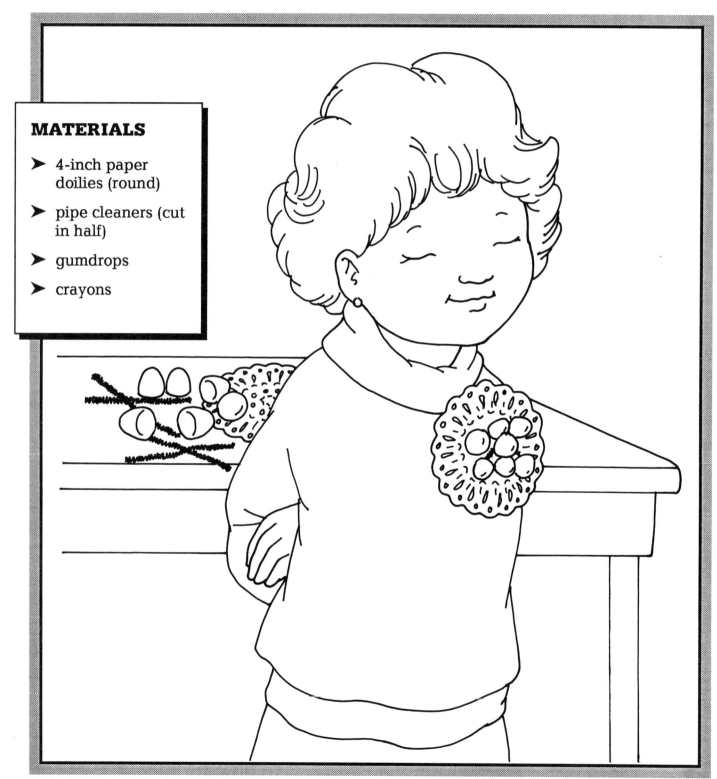

SHARING TOGETHER

➤ What makes a holiday special? Which holidays do you celebrate during the winter? (Be sure to remain sensitive to all religious and cultural holidays during the winter season.) Can you tell us how you celebrate the winter holidays with your family? Do you eat special foods during the winter holidays? What special foods do you eat? Do you set the table in a special way to celebrate the winter holidays? How?

WORKING TOGETHER

Invite the children to make a winter holiday bouquet. Give each child a paper doily. Place the other materials listed on page 54 on a work table within easy reach of the children. Suggest that the children use crayons to color the different sections of their doilies. Then help the children carefully punch several pipe cleaners through the center portion of their doilies. Show the children how to place a gumdrop on the end of each of the pipe cleaners to form a cluster. Demonstrate for the children how the bouquet can be worn as a corsage. Encourage the children to take their winter holiday bouquets home to share with their families.

A Holiday Container

MATERIALS

➤ clean coffee or peanut cans with lids (ask the children to bring these from home)

➤ construction paper in a variety of colors

➤ marking pens or crayons

➤ glitter, rickrack, buttons, ribbon, yarn, and any other decorative materials

➤ scissors

➤ glue

SHARING TOGETHER

➤ Do you have a favorite snack or treat? What is it? Can you name some healthy treats? Can you name some special winter holiday treats? What are your favorite treats during the winter holidays?

WORKING TOGETHER

Before beginning this activity, cut the construction paper into squares. Invite the children to gather together around a large work table. Place the materials listed on page 56 within easy reach of the children. Help the children glue different colors of construction-paper squares in an overlapping design on their cans. Encourage the children to add details to their holiday containers with glitter, ribbon, and other decorative materials. Suggest that the children take their finished containers home and ask their families to fill the containers with healthy winter holiday treats. You may want to serve a treat in one of the holiday containers at snacktime, too.

Valentine Friendship Tree

MATERIALS

- ➤ squares of red construction paper
- ➤ yarn
- ➤ paper punch
- ➤ marking pens
- ➤ scissors
- ➤ tree branch
- ➤ white spray paint (optional)
- ➤ container of sand

SHARING TOGETHER

➤ Can you draw a heart? Which holiday reminds you of hearts? Can you draw the shape of a heart in the air with your finger? Let's try it together. Do you know what a valentine is? A valentine is a special card or gift you give to your friends and family on Valentine's Day.

WORKING TOGETHER

Before beginning this activity, place a tree branch in a container of sand so that the branch stands independently. Spray paint the tree branch white, if desired. Then show the tree branch to the children and explain that they are going to make a Valentine Friendship Tree. Invite the children to make hearts by folding each of the squares of red construction paper in half. Draw half of a heart shape on each fold. Give each child one of the prepared squares and ask an adult volunteer to help the children cut along the drawn lines. Children can open the cut-out shapes to reveal a heart. Ask the adult volunteer to help the children write their names on their heart shapes. Use a paper punch to punch a hole at the top of each heart. Encourage the children to string yarn through the holes and tie the ends of the yarn together. Invite the children to hang their hearts on the Valentine Friendship Tree.

Love Boat Sandwiches

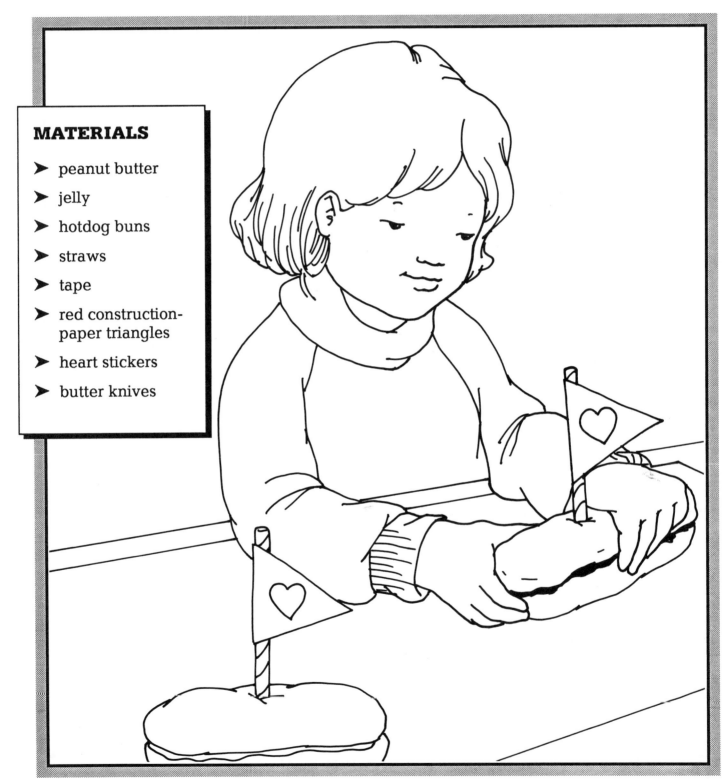

MATERIALS

➤ peanut butter

➤ jelly

➤ hotdog buns

➤ straws

➤ tape

➤ red construction-
   paper triangles

➤ heart stickers

➤ butter knives

SHARING TOGETHER

➤ What is your favorite sandwich? How do you make your favorite sandwich? Can you make a sandwich by yourself? Do you help make sandwiches at home?

➤ Can you make a Love Boat Sandwich out of these ingredients? (Display hotdog buns, peanut butter, jelly, straws, and red triangles.) How do you think we could make sandwiches with these things? (Make a sandwich with the class and display the finished product.)

WORKING TOGETHER

Invite the children to make their own Love Boat Sandwiches. Remind the children to wash their hands and a working surface thoroughly before handling the food items. Place the materials listed on page 60 on the work table within easy reach of the children. Show the children how to spread peanut butter and jelly inside the hotdog buns and stick a straw in the center of each sandwich. Then encourage the children to decorate the red triangles with heart stickers. Tape the decorated triangles on the straws for sails.

Hearty Sandwiches

MATERIALS

➤ red jam

➤ white bread

➤ heart-shape cookie cutters

➤ butter knives

SHARING TOGETHER

➤ What colors remind you of Valentine's Day? What about red? What about white? What is red on Valentine's Day?

➤ Have you ever made heart-shaped cookies? Do you know how to make a jam sandwich? How? Have you ever made a sandwich in the shape of a heart?

WORKING TOGETHER

Invite the children to join you in making heart sandwiches. Remind the children to wash their hands and the surface of a work table before handling the food items. Place the materials listed on page 62 on the work table within easy reach of the children. Show the children how to use heart-shaped cookie cutters to cut hearts from slices of bread. Encourage the children to spread their heart-shaped bread slices with jam and then place another heart-shaped slice on top to make a sandwich. Then enjoy heart sandwiches in valentine colors!

Valentine Treats

MATERIALS

➤ cream cheese

➤ hand mixer or beater

➤ red food coloring (or red juice)

➤ raisins

➤ cherries

➤ bread

➤ heart-shaped cookie cutters

➤ butter knives

➤ tray

SHARING TOGETHER

➤ Do you like to make valentine treats? Which treats do you like to make? Do you like to make special treats with your family? What kinds of special treats have you made with your family?

➤ Do you think you can spread frosting on a valentine cookie? Let's pretend to spread frosting on our cookies together.

WORKING TOGETHER

Invite the children to make special valentine treats. Remind the children to wash their hands and the work table surface thoroughly before handling the food items. Invite the children to watch as you whip the cream cheese with the hand mixer. Then add red food coloring to make the cheese turn pink (you may also add red juice, such as cherry or cranapple). Encourage the children to use heart-shaped cookie cutters to cut bread slices into heart shapes and then spread the pink cream cheese on the bread hearts. Demonstrate how to arrange raisins and cherries on the cream cheese to make faces or designs. Serve the open-face heart sandwiches on trays as a special valentine treat.

Valentine Plates

MATERIALS

➤ heavy-duty paper plates

➤ 1" x 12" strips of tagboard

➤ lace doilies

➤ crayons

➤ glue

➤ stapler

SHARING TOGETHER

➤ Do you celebrate Valentine's Day at home with your family? How? Do you have a special Valentine's Day lunch, dinner, or treat? Do you set the table in a special way? How? Would you like to decorate some plates to use on Valentine's Day?

WORKING TOGETHER

Invite the children to make special plates to use for valentine treats. Give each child a heavy-duty paper plate and a lace doily. Suggest that the children use crayons to decorate the lace doilies and then glue their doilies to the paper plates. Show the children how to draw valentine designs or patterns on 1" x 12" strips of tagboard. Then help the children staple the ends of the decorated tagboard strips to each side of the paper plates to form handles (like a basket). Encourage the children to take their valentine plates home to use for valentine treats.

EXPLORING WINTER THROUGH ART

ART is a fun, productive way of learning all about the winter season. Using different materials, children can make holiday gift wrap and a snowy paperweight, as well as special gifts for Valentine's Day and other winter holidays.

Personalized Gift Wrap

MATERIALS

➤ sheets of plain, white wrapping paper

➤ crayons or marking pens

SHARING TOGETHER

➤ Do you know what a gift is? A gift is something special that you give to someone you care about. Have you ever given a gift to someone? Who did you give a gift to? Did you wrap the gift in wrapping paper? Have you ever received a gift from someone? Was it fun to unwrap your gift? What gift did you get? Tell us about your favorite gift.

WORKING TOGETHER

Before beginning this activity, print each child's name in large letters on separate sheets of plain, white wrapping paper. Then invite the children to find the sheets of wrapping paper with their names printed on them. Encourage the children to trace around the letters of their names with bright crayons or marking pens and then color the remaining parts of their papers with interesting designs. Help the children fold the wrapping paper carefully to take home and share with family members. Suggest to the children that they use their special wrapping paper to wrap gifts for their family and friends during the winter holiday season.

Valentine Cards

MATERIALS

➤ marking pens or crayons

➤ red and pink construction paper

➤ heart stickers or stamps

SHARING TOGETHER

➤ How do you show your family that you care about them? Have you ever made a valentine for someone special? Who did you make a valentine for? Have you ever received a valentine? From whom? We send valentines to friends and family members to tell them that we love them. Who would you like to send a valentine to?

WORKING TOGETHER

Invite the children to make special valentines. Place the materials listed on page 70 on a work table within easy reach of the children. Give each child a piece of red or pink construction paper and demonstrate how to fold the paper in half. Help the children write "I love you" on the insides of the cards and then sign their names. Encourage the children to add designs and stickers to the fronts of their cards for decoration. Suggest to the children that they give their cards to someone special on Valentine's Day.

Heart Felt Picture

MATERIALS

➤ white construction-paper heart shapes

➤ red construction paper

➤ rickrack

➤ glitter

➤ glue

➤ crayons

SHARING TOGETHER

➤ Do you help your family at home? What do you do to help your family? Do you have special chores at home that only you are supposed to do? What are they?

WORKING TOGETHER

Invite the children to make special heart felt pictures. Give each child a white paper heart shape. Place the other materials listed on page 72 on a work table within easy reach of the children. Have the children draw pictures on the paper heart shapes of themselves doing something kind for other people. When the drawings are finished, glue each child's heart shape on a sheet of red construction paper. Print "Helping with My Heart" on the top of each red sheet. Encourage the children to decorate their heart pictures by gluing on glitter and rickrack.

Holiday Candle Holders

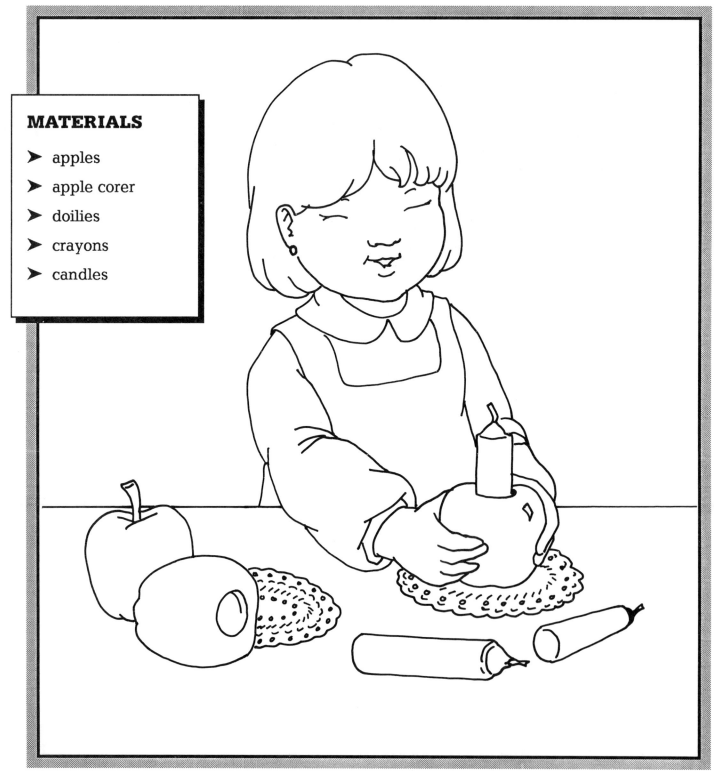

MATERIALS

➤ apples
➤ apple corer
➤ doilies
➤ crayons
➤ candles

SHARING TOGETHER

➤ Do your parents light candles at home on special winter holidays? Raise your hand if you have ever seen a lighted candle. Candles usually cannot stand up by themselves. They need candle holders. (Hold up an apple.) Do you think an apple can be used to hold a candle? Would you like to make a candle holder using an apple?

WORKING TOGETHER

Invite the children to use apples to make special holiday candle holders. Give each child a cored apple, a candle, and a doily. Show the children how to fit their candles into the cored apples. Then invite the children to decorate the doilies. Encourage the children to take their candle holders home and place them on the doilies for a special winter display.

As an alternative activity, children may make the special candle holders out of modeling clay. Use decorative materials, such as buttons, cloth, lace, and sequins, as decoration.

A Snowy Paperweight

MATERIALS

- ➤ a large pitcher of water
- ➤ tablespoons
- ➤ baby food jars
- ➤ small waterproof figures, plastic flowers, and other items (make sure all the items fit inside the baby food jars)
- ➤ waterproof glue
- ➤ glitter
- ➤ electrician's tape
- ➤ newspaper

SHARING TOGETHER

➤ Can you pretend to be a snowflake falling gently to the ground? Let's try it together. Now pretend there is a big wind. Let's be snowflakes blowing in the wind. Oh no! Here comes a really big gust of wind! Let's pretend the wind is blowing us all around. Now the wind is dying down. Let's fall gently to the ground.

WORKING TOGETHER

Invite the children to make a snowy paperweight. If possible, bring a snow scene from home to show the children. Give each child a baby food jar. Place the other materials listed on page 76 on a work table within easy reach of the children. Fill each of the baby food jars with water and add a tablespoon of glitter. Then have an adult volunteer help the children glue waterproof items to the insides of the baby food jar lids. When the glue is completely dry and the figures are secure, screw the lids tightly on the jars. It might be helpful to tape a strip of electrician's tape around the edge of the jar lids to seal them completely. Encourage the children to shake the jars gently. Watch the glitter fall on the figures like snow. Then wrap the jars carefully in newspaper for the trip home.

Bibliography
of Children's Books

Reading good books to children opens up worlds of information and stimulates imaginations! Establish an early love of reading in children by creating positive experiences with these seasonal selections. Use one or more of these books to introduce an activity, as a follow-up to an activity, or for individual use by the children during independent time.

BOOKS TO ENJOY DURING THE WINTER

Cross-Country Cat, Mary Calhoun, William Morrow and Company, 1979.

In the Flaky Frosty Morning, Karla Kuskin, Harper & Row, 1969.

The Mitten, Alvin Tresselt, Lothrop, 1964.

Owl Moon, Jane Yolen, Philomel Books, 1987.

Sky Dragon, Ron Wegen, Greenwillow Books, 1982.

The Snow Parade, Barbara Brenner, Crown Publishers, Inc., 1984.

The Snowy Day, Ezra Jack Keats, Puffin Books, 1962.

A Winter Day, Douglas Florian, Greenwillow Books, 1987.

OTHER BOOKS TO ENJOY THROUGHOUT THE YEAR

Annie and the Wild Animals, Jan Brett, Houghton Mifflin, 1985.

Calico Cat's Year, Donald Charles, Childrens Press, 1984.

First Comes Spring, Anne Rockwell, Crowell, 1985.

Frederick, Leo Lionni, Pantheon, 1967.

Growing Vegetable Soup, Lois Ehlert, Harcourt Brace Jovanovich, 1987.

Haircuts for the Woolseys, Tomie de Paola, Putnam Publishing Group, 1989.

The Little House, Virginia Lee Burton, Houghton Mifflin, 1942.

New Boots for Spring, Harriet Ziefert and Deborah Kogan Ray, Viking Press, 1989.

Ox-Cart Man, Donald Hall, Puffin Books, 1979.

Sunshine Makes the Seasons, Franklyn M. Branley, Crowell, 1974.

A Year in the Country, Douglas Florian, Greenwillow Books, 1989.